50 Reasons to Vote for Donald Trump

B.D. Cooper

ISBN-10: 151765811X
ISBN-13: 978-1517658113

INTRODUCTION

If you are reading this book, you are probably either curious about Donald Trump as a United States Presidential candidate, or you've already made up your mind that you are a supporter.

I've compiled 50+ reasons why it makes sense to vote for Trump for President. I hope you enjoy this book and that it provides some discussion topics for your own debates.

50 REASONS TO VOTE FOR DONALD TRUMP

1.   Donald Trump is a champion for the middle class.

The middle class in this country is under attack. The middle class is under attack from all sides.   The middle class feels invisible and unheard by most politicians. Trump hears them.

In March 2015 Trump said, "everybody is hitting the middle class and something has to happen because we're not going to have a middle class or the middle class is going to do something that you and I and nobody else is going to like and who can blame them? They are getting decimated."

In the second Republican debate Trump touched on his new tax plan (yet to be published at the time of the debate), describing it as it a "major reduction for the middle class." His plan is all about "reducing taxes for the middle class". He is the candidate to save the middle class.

2.   Trump is a job creator.

"I will be the greatest jobs President that God ever created," he said.

"I'll bring back our jobs and I'll bring back our money." This is a claim not to be taken lightly.

A CNN Money analyst[1] calculated that at least 34,000 jobs are attributable to Donald Trump. He has hired more people than any Presidential candidate in the history. The logic follows that if he can create this number of jobs in the private sector he will be able to create many more working for the public sector.

3. Trump is a good businessman.

Not only is Trump a businessman, he is a *good* businessman. Time and time again he has proven himself as a manager and a business owner. He oversees thousands of employees in multiple businesses with diverse interests. Trump said, "I have made the tough decisions, always with an eye toward the bottom line. Perhaps it's time America was run like a business."

Even Texas Senator Ted Cruz acknowledges Trumps business skills. He said in a statement: "His experience as a successful businessman and job creator will prove crucial to ensuring the eventual GOP nominee is not only well-equipped to defeat Hillary Clinton in November, but also to make America great again."

4. He will save Social Security.

Although this may go against the views of some social conservatives, Trump is adamant that America keeps its promises to aging Americans.

In 2000 he said, "Social Security faces a problem: 77 million baby boomers set to retire. Now I know there are some Republicans who would be just fine with allowing these programs to wither and die on the vine. The way they see it, Social Security and Medicare are wasteful 'entitlement programs'. But people who think this way need to rethink their position. It's not unreasonable for people who paid into a system for decades to expect to get their money's worth--that's not an 'entitlement', that's honoring a deal. We as a society must also make an ironclad commitment to providing a safety net for those who can't make one for themselves."

Trump has not backed down from this view and has slammed his fellow Republicans for wanting to cut Social Security.

5. Trump wants to fix the broken mental health care system.

He said, "Let's be clear about this. Our mental health system is broken. It needs to be fixed. Too many politicians have ignored this problem for too long." And he is right. There are glaring flaws in our mental health systems that prevent people from getting the help they so desperately need.

He advocates for expanding treatment programs. "We need to expand treatment programs, because most people with mental health problems aren't violent, they just need help. But for those who are violent, a danger to themselves or others, we need to get them off the street before they can terrorize our communities. This is just common sense." Many Americans agree with him. We need to do a better job at protecting the vulnerable among us.

6. He supports our military.

At a speech he gave on board the USS Iowa on September 15, 2015 Trump said, "We're going to make our military so big, so strong and so great, so powerful that we're never going to have to use it."

Not only does Trump want to grow and support the US military, he wants to better protect them. He plans to change current policies that prevent our military from carrying weapons on US bases and recruiting center. Trump stated, "We train our military how to safely and responsibly use firearms, but our current policies leave them defenseless. To make America great again, we need a strong military. To have a strong military, we need to allow them to defend themselves."

7. Trump supports our veterans.

Trump has reached out to veterans and veterans' groups across the nation. He has created a hotline and a specific email address where veterans can share their stories and offer suggestions on how to reform the Veterans Administration. He has repeatedly blasted the Obama administration for its failure to provide adequate healthcare for veterans. Veterans for a Strong America, a group that has come under scrutiny in recent days, has also endorsed Trump.

At a speech he gave on board the USS Iowa on September 15, 2015 he promised veterans that they would get "the greatest service of any veterans in any country, because you deserve it."

8. He is a strong supporter of gun rights.

On September 18th of 2015, Donald Trump released his second policy paper outlining his support for expansive gun rights. On his website he states, "The Second Amendment to our Constitution is clear. The right of the people to keep and bear Arms shall not be infringed upon. Period." He later says, "Law-abiding people should be allowed to own the firearm of their choice. The government has no business dictating what types of firearms good, honest people are allowed to own." He will work to protect the second amendment and gun owner rights.

9. He advocates for a National Right To Carry Law.

Most Republican candidates support gun rights, but Trump takes the bold step of pushing for every law-abiding citizen in the US to have the right to carry a concealed weapon. At this time the Right To Carry law is now determined on a state-by-state basis. Donald Trump will change this. He said, "That permit should be valid in all 50 states. A driver's license works in every state, so it's common sense that a concealed carry permit should work in every state. If we can do that for driving – which is a privilege, not a right – then surely we can do that for concealed carry, which is a right, not a privilege."

10. He will get tough with Iran.

Trump has repeated slammed President Barack Obama's nuclear deal with Iran, calling it disgraceful and incompetent. Although he does not like President Barack Obama's nuclear deal, he would not rescind it. This is in direct contrast to what many of the other candidates say they would do. Don't get him wrong, Trump feels the contract is not in our best interest - but he would not just rip it up. Instead he told NBC's Meet The Press, "You know, I've taken over some bad contracts. I buy contracts where people screwed up and they have bad contracts," he said. "But I'm really good at looking at a contract and finding things within a contract that, even if they're bad, I would police that contract so tough that they don't have a chance. As bad as the contract is, I will be so tough on that contract."

11. He would repeal Obamacare.

Hating Obamacare does not make Trump unique among conservatives. All the Republican candidates say they would replace Obamacare if elected. But Trump will replace this failed program with something better. He believes in a universal healthcare system.

As far back as 1999 he said, "I would put forward a comprehensive health care program and fund it with an increase in corporate taxes." Again, he has not backed down from his support of universal healthcare, saying he would negotiate with hospitals to broker the best healthcare plans and so that we as a nation can take care of the poor.

12. Trump wants to rebuild America's crumbling infrastructure.

America's infrastructure is crumbling. Roads need to be repaired, bridges need to be built. In May 2015, following the tragic Philadelphia Amtrak crash, Trump hammered America's "horrible infrastructure" and said: "We have to rebuild our infrastructure: our bridges, our roadways, our airports." Yes, this means more spending, but don't worry, because "Nobody can do that like me. Believe me." He possesses the knowledge and skills needed to rebuild our infrastructure.

13. He is not politically correct, and that's a good thing!

A recent Rasmussen Group[2] poll showed that a large number of Americans agree with Trump that the country has become too "politically correct" and we should accept more honest characterizations of America, including its social, political and economic condition. The survey of 1,000 adults found that 71 percent believe that political correctness is a problem in the US, while only 18 percent disagree. Trump seems to understand this point of view perfectly. He has pulled no punches when debating his Republican opponents. And although some see his comments as offensive, many applaud his disregard for established campaign rules of engagement. It is time to stop letting political correctness get in the way of truth.

14. His hair will go with him to the White House.

It could practically run for office on its own. It may take a lot of hairspray but it is no toupee. It is all the Donald. Who wouldn't want to see that gorgeous head of hair in the White House? (Ok, gotcha on this one! Trump has actually stated that if elected, he will change his famous hairstyle, because it takes too long to take care of every day.)

15. He will build a wall to protect the US southern border.

Americans need to feel safe within our nations borders and right now many don't. Building a wall between the US-Mexican borders has been the cornerstone of Trump's political campaign. If elected, he would erect the wall to help stop the flood of illegal immigrants into the US through Mexico.

Here is what Trump had to say. "I would build a great wall. And nobody builds walls better than me, believe me. And I'll build them very inexpensively. I will build a great wall on our southern border and I'll have Mexico pay for that wall." "You don't have to build it in every location. There would be some locations where you would have guards, where you don't need it because the topography acts as its own wall, whether that's water or very rough terrain."

16. He is tough on immigration.

Donald Trump has a very detailed plan on how deal with the illegal immigration problem that is plaguing the US. His 6-page immigration plan[3] is more thorough and comprehensive than any of the other Republican candidates. It has three core principles:

1. A nation without borders is not a nation. There must be a wall across the southern border.

2. A nation without laws is not a nation. Laws passed in accordance with our Constitutional system of government must be enforced.

3. A nation that does not serve its own citizens is not a nation. Any immigration plan must improve jobs, wages and security for all Americans.

His plan lays out specific strategies for each of the principles. For example, he plans on tripling the number of ICE workers and he will end birthright citizenship (the children born in the US but born to illegal immigrants, also known as anchor babies, would no longer be granted citizenship).

17. He isn't afraid to speak his mind.

This goes along with Trump not being politically correct; Americans respect someone who speaks his or her mind. Unlike most of the candidates, Trump does not have handlers that dictate his words and actions; this allows him to speak freely, unrehearsed. He may be brash, controversial, and often misunderstood but Trump allows voters to see who he really is and it is refreshing.

18. He is a DC outsider.

Trump is the anti-politician. He has absolutely no political experience. Dwight Eisenhower was our last president who won without having ever run for a political office before. Trump is unencumbered by the games and corrupt antics from inside the beltway. Americans are drawn to an outsider who can come in and fix what is wrong inside Washington DC.

19. He will hit ISIS hard.

ISIS is running amuck in the Middle East and threatening our safety here in the US. Many Americans fear the next big terrorist attack on US soil will come from ISIS. Thus far Obama's efforts to combat ISIS have been completely ineffective. Trump has promised that as president he "would knock out the source of their wealth, the primary sources of their wealth, which is oil." Trump told MSNBC, "And in order to do that, you would have to put boots on the ground. I would knock the hell out of them, but I'd put a ring around it and I'd take the oil for our country."

20. He will demand more from Saudi Arabia.

The United States and Saudi Arabia have a longstanding relationship. It is built on a common desire for security and stability in the Middle East but many believe the relationship is too one sided. Trump calls for a more equitable relationship want Riyadh to contribute more for remaining under our protection.

"They make a billion dollars a day," "Saudi Arabia, if it weren't for us, they wouldn't be here," Trump said on Meet The Press. "They wouldn't exist." "They should pay us," "Like it or don't like it, people have backed Saudi Arabia. What I really mind though is we back it at tremendous expense. We get nothing for it."

21. He supports women's rights.

Donald Trump gets a bad rap when it comes to his views towards women. But his views towards women's rights and women's reproductive rights are much more moderate and reasonable than most of the Republican candidates. In the past Trump considered himself pro-choice but has since become pro-life. He has shown a willingness to evolve and learn. Trump told Bloomberg News in January of 2015 that he believes abortion should be banned at some point in pregnancy, with exceptions for rape, incest or life of the mother.

Many feel that the abortion debate should be let go. They believe it will not play a significant role in this election and extremists, on either end, will not fare well.

In an interview with the Daily Beast[4], Susan Del Percio, a Republican strategist, said that at the end of the day it is highly unlikely that reproductive rights would define this election. She did say, however, that candidates perceived as too extreme may alienate women and named Texas Senator Ted Cruz as likely too conservative to gain traction with women nationwide.

22. Trump would ban lobbyists from his administration.

Many Americans rightfully feel that lobbyists have far too much power. They are the King Makers in DC. Most candidates are deeply indebted to lobbyists. Trump's relationship with lobbying would be a refreshing change. "I would certainly have a ban," he said on Meet the Press. "You can't put a lifetime ban. But you can certainly make it three, four years." Lobbyists have "power that they shouldn't have," he said. "They're going to control whoever's in," referring to "the lobbyists and the special interests and the donors."

23. He is a bold leader.

Voters are sick and tired of the status quo. They want a bold leader who will shake up the establishment. They want a bold leader. Trump is not afraid to stand up to people; he is proving it now in the Republican debates. As President he can use this same boldness to stand up for America.

24. Trump is the master at making a deal.

He is well known for his negotiating skills. He is the author of *The Art of Making the Deal.* The art of negotiation is a necessary skill for a president to have. It will be vital in shaping both domestic and foreign policies.

Trump is rightfully confident in his ability to broker the best deals. He said, "Deals are my art form. Other people paint beautifully on canvas or write wonderful poetry. I like making deals, preferably big deals. That's how I get my kicks." As an incredibly successful businessmen Trump knows how to negotiate and get what he wants. He can do the same for America.

25. Donald Trump is stone cold sober!

Who knew that he was a teetotaler? He may have a lot of vices but heavy drinking is not one of them. He learned to avoid the temptations of alcohol from his brother. "I learned a lot from my brother, Fred," Trump told Forbes in 2011. "He set an example. It wasn't, maybe, the example that people would think, but it really was, in its own way, an example. That here was this fantastic guy, who got caught up in the alcohol, and he ultimately died from alcoholism." Perhaps that bit of restraint and self-control is quality to be admired in a president.

26. Trump advocates a beautifully simple tax plan.

If elected President, Trump plans to simplify the tax code. Trump said, "When they talk about fixing the tax, it's so complicated, that people have to go and use H&R Block to do a $50,000 [return] — a man who makes $50,000 has to spend money."

The US tax code is so complicated that most Americans cannot prepare their own tax returns. Americans spend 6.1 billion hours a year doing their taxes. In 1913, the entire tax law was 27 pages. It is now over 9,000 bloated pages. Trump will simplify taxes.

Trump has not released his tax plan, but if his 2011 plan is any indicator, it may look something like this.

- Up to $30,000, you should pay 1%;
- From $30,000 to $100,000, you should pay 5%;
- From $100,000 to $1 million, you should pay 10%; and
- On $1 million or above, you should pay 15%.

27. He has a reasonable stance on same-sex marriage.

Of all contenders on the Republican side Trump is the most realistic and pragmatic when it comes to gay marriage. "Some people have hopes of passing amendments, but it's not going to happen," he said. "Congress can't pass simple things, let alone that. So anybody that's making that an issue is doing it for political reasons. The Supreme Court ruled on it."

Trump has repeatedly said that he is not for gay marriage but he understands that it is a dead issue. He is a supporter of some gay rights, and believes that a person's sexual orientation is not a valid reason for an employee to be let go.

28. He would renegotiate NAFTA.

The North American Free Trade Agreement, or NAFTA, is an agreement among the United States, Canada and Mexico designed to remove tariff barriers and increase trade between the three countries. Although many economists are fans of NAFTA the American public is less enamored.

Trump echoes many Americans opinions, "I think NAFTA's been a disaster. I think our current deals are a disaster. I'm a free trader, the problem with free trade is you need smart people representing you we have the greatest negotiators in the world, but we don't use them, we use political hacks and diplomats. We use the wrong people..."

29. His stance on climate change.

Trump questions whether or not what we do here in the US really has much of an impact on climate change. Why should we have restrictions in place that adversely affect our economy if it does not solve the problem?

The US cannot solve global warming on its own. Trump explained, "Well of course I'm being sarcastic you know... (but) it's a little bit serious, there's a little bit of seriousness there. Look, we are restricting our factories much more than China, I go to China. They have factories that are much more competitive, I'm not saying friendly, but they're certainly not environmentally friendly. I'm a huge believer in clean air, I'm not a huge believer in the global warming phenomenon..."

30. He will make America great again.

According to the Pew Research Center[5] 49% of the general public and 76% of Conservatives believe that "the country's best years are behind us." Trump plans to change this; he will make America great again.

He has said, "I will not let China rip us off any longer, I will take back jobs from all these places that are killing us including Mexico, who I have great respect for, but I will make our country great again... We have to take it back, we have to take our country back. We've lost our jobs, we've lost our money. We're a third world nation and we're a debtor nation at the same time, you need somebody with the kind of thinking- I built a great company. I have some of the great assets of the world. And I talk about only form- not bragging- I talk about it because that's the kind of mentality that this country needs. We need that mentality now and we need it fast."

"The American Dream is dead. But if I get elected President I will bring it back bigger and better and stronger than ever before and we will make America great again."

31. He will stand up to China.

Many Americans are deeply concerned about China. There is worry about unfair trade agreements and the fact that China owns so much of our debt. Also there is concern over their cyber espionage and their disregard for human rights.

Trump promises to stand up to China. He has pledged to "not let China rip us off anymore." With this most recent market crash in China Trump has called for "a big uncoupling" of the US and Chinese economies. "They want our people to starve -- they're taking our business away. They've taken our jobs away," he said. Many feel we need a President who is willing to distance us from China. Trump is willing.

32. He will break OPEC's grip on oil prices.

In his 2011 best seller, *Time to Get Tough*, Trump extolled the virtues of NOPEC (No Oil Producing and Exporting Cartels Act) that would amend the Sherman Antitrust Act to allow the US to sue OPEC for violating antitrust laws. It did not survive Washington politics but if it had, Trump believed it would have allowed the US to bust up the OPEC cartel.

"Imagine how much money the average American would save if we busted the OPEC cartel. Imagine how much stronger economic shape we would be in if we made the Iraqi government agree to a cost-sharing plan that paid us back the $1.5 trillion we've dropped on liberating Iraq."

Perhaps with Trump in office the Act could pass and America would not be at the mercy of OPEC and other oil-rich nations.

33. He is not beholden to the establishment.

Not only is Trump a DC outsider, he is not afraid to push against the Republican establishment. He is confident enough to disagree with GOP. This is good news to everyone who is tired of politics as usual. He appeals to Conservatives on many issues but he is not afraid push against the party when he disagrees with their policies.

34. He is rich.

He has a net worth somewhere between 4 and 10 billion dollars. He has a proven record of managing money. On the night he announced his presidential campaign he told the crowd "I'm really rich...that's the kind of thinking you need for this country. It sounds crass, it's not crass."

Trumps wealth puts him in a unique position. Financially, he does not need the special interest money. He is not in any special interest group's back pocket. He has a proven record of managing money well. He knows how to minimize debt and maximize wealth that knowledge can lead our country out of financial ruin.

35. He is a great orator.

Most people who have seen Trump speak are surprised by what a great public speaker he is. His extemporaneous style of speaking is natural and approachable and quickly puts an audience at ease. He rarely reads from a prepared speech or teleprompter.

"When I speak in front of large crowds, if you read a speech— it's much easier—but you don't get the reaction," Trump told Jimmy Fallon on the Tonight Show. "If you're reading or you have a teleprompter or even looking down all the time at notes, you're not going to get the reaction from the crowd. It's a riskier proposition because when you read you're not going to make any mistake. When you do it just off the cuff, it's a riskier thing but when you get it right, it's a thing of beauty."

36. He is tough on crime.

Trump will crack down on violent criminals. "We need to get serious about prosecuting violent criminals. The Obama administration's record on that is abysmal. Violent crime in cities like Baltimore, Chicago, and many others is out of control. Drug dealers and gang members are given a slap on the wrist and turned loose on the street. This needs to stop."

"Several years ago there was a tremendous program in Richmond, Virginia called Project Exile. It said that if a violent felon uses a gun to commit a crime, you will be prosecuted in federal court and go to prison for five years – no parole or early release. Obama's former Attorney General, Eric Holder, called that a "cookie cutter" program. That's ridiculous. I call that program a success. Murders committed with guns in Richmond decreased by over 60% when Project Exile was in place – in the first two years of the program alone, 350 armed felons were taken off the street."[6]

37. Donald Trump is world-recognized brand.

He represents the American Dream to the world. Around the world his name is already known and recognized. The US frequently has a branding problem overseas. As President he can help the US manage and promote its brand internationally.

Trump has promised to "take the brand of the United States and make it great again".

38. He is a Christian.

Trump may not be a famous for being super-religious man but he is a Christian. "I believe in God. I am Christian. I think The Bible is certainly THE book." Trump told Christian Broadcasting Network's David Brody in 2011. "First Presbyterian Church in Jamaica Queens is where I went to church. I'm a Protestant, I'm a Presbyterian. And you know I've had a good relationship with the church over the years. I think religion is a wonderful thing. I think my religion is a wonderful religion."

39. Trump plans to tax the rich, including himself.

America is struggling and it needs help. Like Warren Buffet, Trump believes that the ultra-wealthy need to help more. He has proposed a one-time 14.25% tax on the net worth of wealthy Americans.

Trump said, "You've seen my statements. I do very well. I don't mind paying a little more in taxes." He also plans to raise taxes on the wealthy beyond the one-time tax. "I would take carried interest out, and I would let people making hundreds of millions of dollars a year pay some tax, because right now they are paying very little tax and I think it's outrageous."

40. He knows how to deal with the press.

Many Americans are tired of the mainstream media. They are tired of the 24-hour news channels manipulating and spinning the news to suit their own agendas. For many the press has lost all credibly and lacks integrity. Trump repeatedly stands up to the press, and when they push unfairly, he is not afraid to push back.

41. Trump is a builder.

If you are looking for a candidate to rebuild American greatness, then Trump is the obvious choice. He is the only candidate that actually made his career building... Buildings. Trump's organization has built everything from skyscrapers to luxury hotels. He can literally rebuild America.

42. Like the great Ronald Reagan, he is an actor.

Internet Movie Data Base (IMDB) lists 18 acting credits for Donald Trump. Did you know he was in Zoolander? He has also made hundreds of appearances on various talk and reality shows. And you know that is some serious acting. He even won a Razzie in 1991 for his role in the movie *Ghosts Can Do It*.

43. He could stop Russian expansion.

Right now there is an unofficial cold war between America and Russia. Politicians don't know what to do about Putin. Trump is not worried about Russia or Putin. In fact he and Putin share some similarities.

"Well, Putin has no respect for our President whatsoever. He's got a tremendous popularity in Russia. They love what he's doing; they love what he represents. So we have a President who is absolutely…you look at him, the chemistry is so bad between those two people. I was over in Moscow two years ago, and I will tell you, you can get along with those people, and get along with them well. You can make deals with those people. Obama can't."

When Bill O'Reilly asked Trump if he could make a deal with Putin to stop Russia's expansion, Trump replied, "I would, I would be willing to bet I would have a great relationship with Putin. It's about leadership."

44. He is low risk, high reward.

Trump is a gamble that is worth taking. Americans are risk takers. We like to bet on the underdog and despite all his bravado Trump is very much an underdog. When Donald first jumped into the Republican race for President many people thought he was a joke. Now he is leading the polls.

45. Trump won't apologize or back down.

Trump is frequently called on to apologize and he simply won't do it. Trump speaks off the cuff and his words can get him into trouble. Most politicians would back pedal as fast as they could to safe neutral ground. Politician's apologies sound shallow and false to many voters.

Trump refuses to apologize just to please people, even when it could hurt him at the polls. Trump will continue speak his mind and to fire back at people who criticize him.

"I will say what I want to say," Trump said. No apology needed.

46. He will take a tough stance against Mexico.

Our relationship with Mexico is very one-sided. In most of our deals with Mexico America gets the short end of the stick. Americans are tired of it and want a President who will put America's interests first. Trump will.

Trump said, "To the citizens of the United States, who I will represent far better than anyone else as President, the Mexican government is not our friend...and why should they be when the relationship is totally one-sided in their favor on both illegal immigration and trade. I have pointed this out during my speeches and it is something Mexico doesn't want me to say. In actuality, it was only after my significant rise in the polls that Univision, previously my friend, went ballistic. I believe that my examples of bad trade deals for the United States was of even more concern to the Mexican government than my talk of border security."

"The last thing Mexico wants is Donald Trump as President in that I will make great trade deals for the United States and will have an impenetrable border — only legally-approved people will come through easily."

47. Trump is very confident.

Sure some say overconfident. But it takes a lot of confidence to be the leader of the free world. Trump is very good at promoting Trump. He is known for saying: "I did very well." "Nobody knows politicians better than I do." "I get along with everybody." "I get the biggest crowds, "I get the biggest receptions." His confidence makes him seem impervious to criticism. Our next President needs to have the confidence to lead.

48. He is an incredibly hard worker.

Trump is a famous workaholic. As president he would work tirelessly to rebuild America. There will be no long trips to Hawaii or days spent on the golf course if he were Commander in Chief.

In describing a workaholic and who he would like to have work for him, Trump told the New York Post in 2007, "They don't want to miss what's going on. Although vacations are supposed to be about de-stressing, some people admitted it would be more stressful not knowing what was going on at work while they were away. And those are the kind of people I want working for me."

49. Trump is likeable.

The Donald is a very likeable guy. He has a charisma that draws people in. Much like Obama he is very comfortable with himself and that draws people to him. Even people that disagree with Trump on issues feel he has a likeability that most candidates lack.

50. He could beat Hillary.

Trump is electable, Hillary is not. Hillary is a strong candidate with years of experience but she does not draw voters. Many Americans find her very competent but distant and cold. Quite simply, she is not likeable. Trump gets people. He gets Middle America. He is charismatic and speaks a simple truth that has broad appeal. Perhaps Donald got it right when he said, "The last person she [Hillary Clinton] wants to face is Donald Trump."

51. He might actually win.

Early in Trump's campaign, most people thought that Trump's presidential bid was a complete joke. But despite low expectations he has continued to gain support and has emerged as the Republican front-runner.

According to a New York Times/ CBS News Poll[7], Republicans are losing confidence in traditional candidates. Many believe that Donald Trump may have the best chance of winning the presidency in 2016. The poll found that 39 percent of Republican primary and caucus voters viewed Trump as their best shot at winning the presidency, compared with 26 percent in a CBS survey in August. Only 15 percent said they would not back him as the party's standard-bearer.

DID YOU ENJOY THIS BOOK?

I want to thank you for purchasing and reading this book. I really hope you got a lot out of it.

Can I ask a quick favor though?

If you enjoyed this book I would really appreciate it if you could leave me a positive review on Amazon. This is huge (huuuuuge) for helping other readers find this book and decide if it is a good purchase.

Leave a review and let me know which of the 50 reasons is your favorite.

SOURCES

1.   http://money.cnn.com/2015/09/03/news/economy/donald-trump-jobs-created/

2.   http://www.rasmussenreports.com/public_content/politics/general_politics/august_2015/is_america_too_pc

3.   https://www.donaldjtrump.com/positions/immigration-reform

4.   http://www.thedailybeast.com/articles/2015/08/14/can-any-republican-win-the-women-s-vote.html

5.   http://www.people-press.org/2014/06/26/section-2-views-of-the-nation-the-constitution-and-government/

6.   https://www.donaldjtrump.com/positions/second-amendment-rights

7.   http://www.nytimes.com/interactive/2015/09/15/us/politics/document-poll-presidential-race.html?_r=2